Soul You Vol. III

THE PROTECTOR

Soul You Vol. III: The Protector. Copyright 2021 by Sherika Frazier Duncan. All rights reserved. No part of this publication may be reproduced, distributed, or transmitted in any form or by any means, including photocopying, recording, or other electronic or mechanical methods, without the prior written permission of the publisher, except in the case of brief quotations embodied in critical reviews and certain other noncommercial uses permitted by copyright law. For permission requests, write to the publisher, addressed "Attention: Permissions Coordinator," 3819 Ulmer Court, Tallahassee, FL 32311.

Sherika Duncan books may be purchased for educational, business or sales promotional use. For information, please email the Sales Department at sales@sherikaduncan.com.

First Edition Printed, February 2021
Library of Congress Cataloging-in-Publication Data has been applied for.
ISBN: 978-1-7364355-2-6

CONTENTS

Plight 1
   Dependency & Complacency 1
   Being Courageous 2
   Expectations 4
Self-Identity 5
   About self 5
   About life 5
   Rites of passage 5
Relationships 7
   Being honest and trustworthy 11
   Past Relationships guarded 11
   Being patient 11
   Internal Healing 11
Self-Worth 14
Take Back Our Land 16
Asar 17
Mansa Musa of Mali 19
Kush 24
Alexander the Great 26
Shaka Zulu 27
Maya Inca Aztec Civilization 29
King Solomon 32
Abraham Lincoln 34
Black Wall Street 35
Human Zoo 37
Ota Benga 38
Dr. Martin L. King, Jr. 40
Public Housing Plan & Drugs 42
Malcom X 43
Dr. Wesley Muhammad 44

This book is a love letter to assist in your daily struggles as a black king, your very own survival kit, and a guide on leading you through your path.

Take back our lands and become a village again and raise the babies. We must change our hoods back into neighborhoods, get to know our neighbors, and gain value and respect. To get back to where we left off, what are you willing to do? It is not the American dream. It is the indigenous people's dream to be more like the indigenous people. Time, energy, resource, and wealth of info are priceless.

These books are based on the reader's consciousness level to gravitate and build more curiosity about life and your purpose found inside this material.

Dedicated to my son,
Nyles J'Sean Duncan
with love.

Plight

African variety was the initial reason our power declined so rapidly. Endocrine language has put a spell on communicating in other ways without using their programmed language after learning ABC's fundamentals. It was not a motherland to misunderstand each distinct language. Multiple languages pulled us apart as a whole and started to identify one from another.

It was the beginning of discovering the many unique groups of people. The detachment caused suffering being isolate from each other because we long interconnectedness amongst each other.

We are more powerful united. It is coincidental how today's society is telling us to separate and stay at home. It is the reason for our massive loss of life in this season.

Dependency & Complacency

European Ideology dominance was inflicted upon our people. Territorial ambition unfolded the institutional control, aka constitution of the founding fathers will rule over the people and be slaves of their opinions, ideas, and teachings. The lack of strong, direct, and action-oriented force was highly promoted in American history books about the African Man. It was used as a psychological method to repetitiously remind us of how they wanted us to perceive ourselves by killing the productive male image and instill avoidance of rebellion and encourage fear by taking away our native language.

Being Courageous

More than ever, you are taking personal accountability by being courageous and resilient to your inner voice and beliefs. We rebelled and resisted enslavement every step of the way. Here are just a few of many factual slave narratives of courageous efforts shown by our ancestors. You are putting your freedom first and commanding your needs.

There was a legal act **called The Meritorious Manumission Act of 1710** during the enslavement period in Virginia of freeing an enslaved African for "good deeds. Good deeds were defined as snitching to save a life of a white racist colonial enslaver or his property, invented something from which a white racist colonial enslaver could make a profit, or "snitched" on a fellow enslaved African who was planning a rebellion or to run away. Africans "snitched" to provide the white racist colonial enslaver information that enabled him to abort the revolution and kill the leaders.

Nicholas Owens published a 120-page autobiography of his experience as a slave dealer from 1746 to 1757 on the Coast of Africa and America entitled Journal of a slave dealer. He wrote about the slave trade to prosper and his association in a revolt, and the inevitable capture of people's ship and death by natives of Sierra Leone.

In 1763 Berbice Guyana, the slaves became tired of their oppressors' abusive treatment, the Dutch masters. The uprising slaves became hostile. Two rebellious slaves named **Cuffy** and **Akara** led a practical training, then successfully defeated and took over the southern part of Berbice.

In 1750, **John Newton** was a captain of slave ships, and after retiring, he became an investor in the slave trade. Years later, he was an ordained clergyman who wrote hymns such as Amazing Grace then converted into an abolitionist to support getting rid of slavery. He mentioned slave revolts on board ships were frequent. The slaves were always waiting for the opportunity to succeed an entire ship should one good minute or hour of not effectively surveillance occurs.

Gabriel Crosser headed an uprising in 1800 but did not have enough supplies.

Jean-Jacques Dessalines, one of Louverture's generals and himself a former slave, led the revolutionaries at the Battle of Vertieres on November 18, 1803, where the French forces were defeated. On January 1, 1804, Dessalines declared the nation independent and renamed it Haiti. The Haitian revolution on an island was their grand weaponry. By successfully defeating Napoleon, Spain's England, and the united states army, they formed their own independent country. It is why they are economically challenged as payback due to their successes from humiliating the other countries.

Nat Turner's revolt killed between fifty-five and sixty-five people, at least fifty-one of Caucasians, in 1831. The revolution was put down in a few days. However, Turner remained in hiding for more than two months, which eventually led to stricter state legislation on revolts and freed and rebels' execution.

In 1841, **Solomon Northup**, a free-born New York violinist, was tricked into traveling to Washington DC for more work by two Caucasian men who kidnapped him and took him to

New Orleans to be sold for $650 into slavery for 12 years. We were not passive or submissive to slavery. A terrible day of revenge will come in your favor.

The most successful slave revolt happened in 1841, led by **Madison Washington**. There were seven disgruntle fellow slaves motivated to rebel. They murdered a slave trader and took control of the Creole by wounding his crew to sail to Nassau. It was a British colony in the United Kingdom where they abolished slavery in 1833. The Americans protested, yet the British empire granted the slaves free and ignored the protest efforts.

Frederick Douglas spoke of how to revolt, rebel, and resist the attempts at slavery in 1852.

Expectations

- To know there are harsh criminal sentences for certain now legal decriminalized drugs.

- Based on society's perception of black men, black men are subject to unjust criminal punishment.

- Our young black kings will be disproportionately assigned to highly challenging inside the classroom.

- The race itself is a way to send manipulative dehumanizing messages regarding several intensifying statements about people's differences.

- We must overcome through a matter of fact, and direct engagements that regularly display judgmental views of skin color can damage the world's perspectives describing each other and risk the collaborative relationship.

Self-Identity

About self
The predecessor of light born of the heat of the galaxy you were formed. Black is king; In Western civilization, you had so much stolen from you, including your African names. In Yoruba culture, your birth name is seriously overemphasized because of the belief that it will affect you throughout your entire life. Your childhood exposure plays a significant influence on being exposed to various activities or places through extracurricular activities such as sports and music, family vacations, and parents' work settings had on your development. The opportunity to travel abroad and to witness your parents working self-employed or in other professional settings expanded your outlook on the future.

About life
Family outcomes of being on welfare or working-class experiencing police racial profiling and growing up in at-risk neighborhoods will make you culturally aware. Your mother's romantic relationship posed as the biological father into the dad's role will cause unsupportive actions from within. Because she continues to put her sons on a cycle of temporary male father figures due to your father's absence increases antisocial behavior, at-risk students, it is critical to find ways to improve high-school performance.

Rites of passage
These interventions emphasize the importance of African and African American history and culture to raise the critical consciousness and critical thinking of African American male youth related to a legacy of success. The only obstacles holding

Black men back are preparation, knowledge, education, and your quality in manhood development. Black champions in our communities and the Black media representatives must tell actual compelling narratives about Black people made or contributing outcomes every day. Black men's emphasis is to bring attention to mentors' necessity to help Black boys narrow the country's achievement gap. You must build our young men up to make sure they are on point;

Our government and society, in general, continue to ensure you fail and experience challenges while climbing from the bottom to the top. The educational system was structured differently for Blacks by shortening the school durations to accommodate black children expected to work when planting, harvesting, carrying cement, laying rails, and loading and unloading freight obligations. The operation is set up for Black males to slip, and it is tough to rise from the bottom to the top. You can start working to improve our community by spreading love instead of friction between each other.

Please remember who you are because you can't wear a crown with your head hanging down.

RELATIONSHIPS

Allow yourself to date her as if you are on a job interview by not boasting to your friends about intimate details. This could damage her reputation, or you may entice your supposedly good friend to finesse his way and approach her for himself. Her past is her past.

What do you require?

> *What were you doing for yourself before you met me?*
>
> *How much were you sexing?*
>
> *How often were you talking to Jodie?*
>
> *How often were you getting your hair and nails done?*
>
> *How often would you like it done?*

When you discover she a no-nonsense type of woman, try to keep calm and not edgy. You can coexist with your partner and allow her an opportunity to grow and learn together. She can always tell if you are interested. Should you discover a need or a want, she has in mind, protect and provide, and be willing to help. If your hygiene is not as up to par, be humble and allow your woman to build you up as you discover new ways to take care of your hygiene. Women see us as the catalyst, good men. We are good listeners.

Our queen is our peace. She is our portal Protect her heart.

Your woman is not your homeboy.

It's ok to release feminine energy around your woman when you say you love her should solidify their place. Women need constant reassurance and attention. You must talk more, at the beginning of your relationship, to build trust in each other.

Know your woman's trauma at the beginning

Maybe your woman has abandonment issues. Communication is key. Get into her mind.

What is her relationship like with her family?

Love on your energy king

You can express everything you desire from a relationship. If you only want to love on the woman's body with no strings attached, then be exact. If you don't have any plans to love her, do not disturb her energy because she can send negative energy in your direction. She is saying she hate that nigger, and it's hurting your life. She can think negatively about you, and her thoughts more robust enough will manifest in your reality. Her mind is mighty which she can cast a lot of spells on you.

Treat women like God be respectful, patient, appreciative as if He came and visited right now. If you love her, then king, you must pray for her protection, health, mind, and spirit.

You want a superwoman but you, not a superman.

Because you love God and mesmerize that God even thought about you, that's how you should treat women speak in their environment everywhere a woman goes; it's her environment. A woman can enter a room full of men, and suddenly there occurs an automatic energy shift due to the men feeling her presence. Treat women with the same respect and amount of love. When you have a good woman in your life, you pray and thank God.

The safest place on earth is with your woman.

Because you just love God and mesmerize that God even thought about you, that's how you should treat women speak in their environment everywhere a woman goes; it's her environment. A woman can enter a room full of men, and suddenly there occurs an automatic energy shift due to the men feeling her presence. Treat women with the same respect and amount of love. When you have a good woman in your life, you pray and thank God. The safest place on earth is with your woman. You can refrain from being so reactive to your woman. Because she told you about yourself, and you lash out at her, then unexpectedly force yourself upon this woman and hit her. Then later, you want to talk to God.

How you treat women reflects what's going on in your body, your mind, and heart?

Everything matters, leave the Ego and change your posture be soft and be at peace by taking control when required. You don't have to have power in all situations and be dominant. Stops being so right all the time to prevent conflict in the relationship. It's not she thinks she's right but thinks she is not wrong. If she is sure you are in control over your mind now, she will know you are a responsible man and will submit. When a woman can be a woman, it lets you be a man. Men lead, but a woman is leading right there with you. She is driving it with you. The more she can trust your leadership role, the more she can be submissive, and she can tap into her feminine energy. If she wants to argue, then it's for a reason. She is not sure you can handle it. Men can't take what they put out. You can't feel the way a woman can handle that a woman's mindset is different. When you told her to shut up, it was cool, but when she tells you to shut up, it's a problem. A woman will give you that reflection. She is going to provide you with precisely what you give her. She has no time restriction. You did it last year, and she sits back and does it to you five years later. That made her feel she wasn't significant in your life, like she was a burden.

Why do you have an attraction towards other people?

Animals exude natural laws in the universe; spend time observing animals in natural habitats to understand life balance on a higher level. The male lion in the pride attracts the female lions to the tribe certain male lions attract to join his pride. There is a whole vibration of femininity and masculinity, such as feminine arousing masculine energy. Certain people are embedded in alpha or beta energy and or alpha and omega energy. Certain people who are abnormal to their originality, such as celebrity stars, pull each other closer. Black holes are like vacuums because of the pull of lights. We must successfully attempt to take what's in our minds and process and analyze our thoughts, actions, and energy.

SELF-REFLECTION

Being honest and trustworthy
Communication is essential for you and your woman to understand and with judgment, Ego, and fear.

Past Relationships guarded
You are looking for a woman to play her gender role and respect her culture and know her internal worth to this world. She knows she is a descendant of the pharaoh.

Being patient
You must learn patience. For example, you are interested in a beautiful black queen, yet your delivery is off. You must be mindful of how you treat her, especially one who is in sports that appear masculine until it's too late and she ends up in the arms of a white man. The white man might be the valuable person at the time in her life. Therefore, she went to where the value was in the white man. You can't get mad if someone else acknowledges your black queen.

> *Did you see your dad value your mom?*
> *Did you see your mom value your dad?*
> *Did you see your mom and or dad value our culture?*

Internal Healing
Our heart should be drawn to the truth of ancient Egypt. Black people were the most spiritual and intellectual people of all time in ancient Egypt. We must acknowledge the fact and see it within ourselves. Respect and value the black woman. When she shows distress, we can play the role by caressing.

MASLOW'S HIEARCHY OF NEEDS

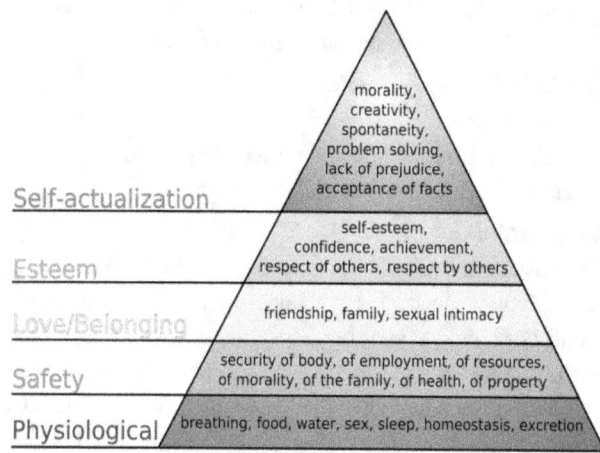

MASLOW'S MOTIVATION MODEL

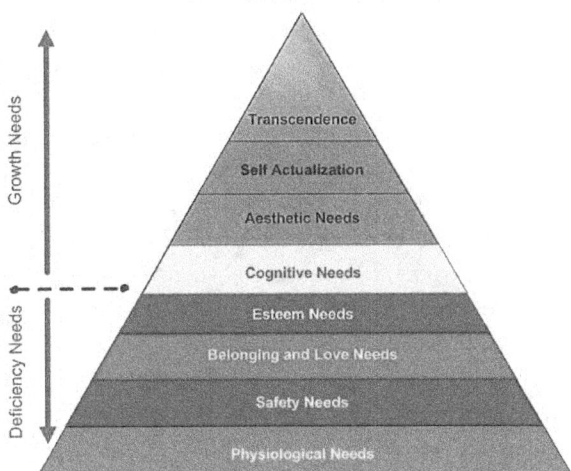

SELF-WORTH

Your self-worth is your power. Adding value to the world, connect more with the Earth. While the sun hits your skin, reprogram your mind by being open-minded to receiving information. Blacks don't get cancer from the sun four to six hours of sun daily compared to Caucasian thirty minutes to one hr. You must connect more with the Earth as the sun hits your skin. The ground pulls terrible energy from the bottom of your soles when you're connected to it. Molecules make up atoms, then atoms make up the DNA, Protein Enzymes, and chemicals. It is your chemicals and DNA that make up the organs, which make up your body. It is interconnected to your soul affecting your spiritual body, then your spiritual body is affected by your DNA. You can take cold showers to think about the hair conditioning process rinsing with cold water. You should do this for the entire body to close pores. Hot showers expose fluoride to enter your bloodstream.

Why are natural beings eating unnaturally?

GMO alters your DNA. You didn't come from a lab. You came from netter, aka nature. Remember who you are. Fame represents stars. Don't let this world drive you crazy. A study was conducted called Global Patterns of Linkage Disequilibrium at the CD4 Locus and Modern Human Origins, which depicts Africans. Their descendants possess nine distinct sequences, which are the most sequences among the other races with six and animals with four counts.

Dear King,

If no one has told you lately, then I will...

>I Love You
>
>I Love You
>
>I Love You
>
>I Love You
>
>I Love You
>
>I Love You
>
>I Love You
>
>I Love You
>
>I Love You
>
>I Love You

Take Back Our Land

Yoruba sculpture and art and the architectural advancement under the Sahara Put the work in start small and grow large King move: speak, think, eat, cultivate sow seed do you invest, time, how can you make these moves if you want to be promiscuous smoke instead talk about life from within you by saying, "I am a god," and speak good intentions without compromising.

What do I have to learn from this?
How can this teach me?

Comparing is illusional. Remove those parasites from your circle. The two most essential retrospectives were when you entered this world, and the other is when you made it up in your consciousness to determine why.

Aten- highest level of intelligence for a black man Aten nation Vs. Amen, you put yourself in darkness, Aten, you put yourself in a state of light in mind.

ASAR

Fact or Myth

The name AS-ar relates to the Egyptian word for "prince," or "chief," ser, s. Oser and the most known (Greek version), Osiris. He is described as a green/black skin man with a beard dressed in white mummy wrappings. He holds the crook and flail, the Egyptian symbols of supreme power. Be your per-son percentage of the sun.

This symbolizes your body passing back to earth as you biodegrade before your soul goes back to the solar system. If you even have a soul
The scale of MAAT
Left it's a heart, the right it is a feather.
Not your brain on the scale but
Your heart talks to your brain called cardio neurology.
Whatever the heart intended to do, it commands the body all your actions in life are stored in your heart.

Lesson Learned:

_____

_____

_____

_____

_____

_____

_____

_____

_____

MANSA MUSA OF MALI

Musa Keita Musa Mata, aka Mansa Musa, was born in Mali, West Africa, in c. 1280, and is known as the wealthiest person in all history, with a peak net worth of approximately US$418 billion. Mansa Musa was also referred to as Kanku Musa, who was his mother's name. His father's name was Faga Laye. Mansa Musa had four wives. One of his wives, name was Inari Kunate, was the traveling senior wife of Mansa Musa. He was assigned the name Mansa which signifies King in ancient Mali. Over decades Musa commanded Ghana Empire. The Mali Empire later seized Ghana.

Mansa Musa succeeded in twenty-four municipalities with their territories in Senegal territories, Gambia, Burkina Faso, Mali, Chad, Nigeria, Niger, and Mauritania in West Africa. He executed a world-historical journey during the 1324 trip to Mecca, a traveling range of about 4000 miles. He is said to have traveled along with 60,000 men, including 12,000 slaves, of which each one of them brought 2kgs of gold bars and heralds covered in silks who bore gold staffs, provided horses, and managed bags.

He utilized slaves to care for his wealth, although it was told he was a cheerful giver to all the land, which seemingly included slaves. Musa was equipped to put in place all the essentials for the cavalcade. He accomplished to feed all the men and mammals, including more than eighty camels, each carrying between 23kgs and 136kgs of gold dust, gold, copper, and salt. Mansa built a mosque every Friday. Mansa Musa delivered out gold to the two helpless people he met on the route and gave a lot in the cities he crossed on his path to Mecca, including Cairo and Madina's cities. He reportedly exchanged gold for keepsakes.

But Musa's philanthropic acts inadvertently enormously changed the economics of the counties he moved across. Throughout Cairo, Medina, and Mecca, gold volume penetration reduced metal within the following few years. Commodities and goods prices increased. On his way from Mecca, Mansa Musa borrowed all the gold he possessed from the money-borrowers in Cairo at incredibly massive interest for the first time in Egypt. The value of gold dropped it did not recover for the next twelve years. It became the only time in history for a single person to regulate gold prices in the Mediterranean. Mansa Musa dictated for twenty-five years and died in c. 1337. His son Maghan succeeded him. Musa created institutions and mosques in the area. Niani was Mali's capital city, controlling important trade routes across the Sahara Desert to Europe and the Middle East.

The city of Timbuktu was considered a center for education and learning. Many people later could visit Mali for studies at Sankore University. He is today recognized for his golden age in the history of Mali. His assets are assessed at $400 Billion.

c. 1375 depicts west Africa with Mansa Musa's image holding a large gold nugget catalog atlas was published explorers started visiting to discover the hidden gem to Mansa Musa success. Africa's trajectory was on a full, successful path compared to the Europe trajectory in physical and human resources. Yet the Arabian initiated and European successfully raped us from reaching our goals. We should reflect on our past to learn from the successes and the failures to prevent the same outcomes.

The Mandinka people are in the south of eastern Guinea and north of the Ivory Coast. They are primarily found in the south part of Mali, known as the West African ethnic group. Numbering about 11 million majorities of Mandinka religion is Islam. Their language consists of Mandinka from the Mande language and lingua franca of the West Africa family.

We can't be flashy with our most affluent and most valuable possessions and expect other races not to attempt to rob or destroy us.

Lesson Learned:

_____

_____

_____

_____

_____

_____

_____

_____

_____

Early humans had lived in Africa for numbers of thousands of years as foragers. Nubian and early Egyptian artifacts seemed to have many connections. This symbolizes that the two societies may have experienced many qualities like rulers, inscribed symbols, and innovative features. There is also evidence of organized commerce networks linking Nubia and Egypt.

Nubia was in an area that engaged in the flow of goods like ivory from inner Africa to the Mediterranean region. Nubians lived in stone houses. Archaeologists have found proof of Nubian storage pits, flint deposits, stone instruments, grindstones, gold, copper, and pottery. Some of these artifacts came from local sources, while others came from Egypt and away. Nubians also similarly mummified their dead to the Egyptians. Both societies buried bodies facing west and left sacrifices to guide the dead to the afterlife. Lapis lazuli, a semi-precious, deep blue stone, has also been found, like shown in the picture below, to symbolize fertility.

KUSH

In the northern Africa region of Sudan, a kingdom called Kush is better known as Nubia, derived from the Nubia people or the Egyptian word nub, meaning gold.

Roughly, c. 8,000 BCE Kush kingdom the land referred to Egyptian as the black people's land begins to rise referring to the indigenous people black skin. The Kushites much evolved and were significantly influenced by Egypt. Egypt relied on Kerma to import gold, ebony, incense, exotic animals, and ivory, among other luxury items.

Lesson Learned:

_____

_____

_____

_____

_____

_____

_____

_____

_____

_____

ALEXANDER THE GREAT

In 1611, the King James Bible states that a white man came to save us from a life of sins as docile slaves. So many efforts went into covering up our history.

Alexander the Great removed and burned sacred documents of evidence to cover up our past. Ancient Egypt became unburied from the sands. The artifacts were intentionally damaged by chiseling the statues' noses and lips, particularly the ones with robust African descent features. while pretending it was a white civilization.

SHAKA ZULU

Shaka Senzangakhona, also known as Shaka Zulu, was the King Zulu Kingdom King significant reforms. KwaZulu-Natal South Africa, in July 1787. He was successful in uniting all the ethnic groups in southern Africa against the despicable vestiges of colonialism. He was the illegitimate son, Shaka had created the most powerful kingdom on the south part of Africa's continent. He built the Zulu community into a nation of over a million strong. They were responsible for restructuring the Zulu military as a powerful force.

When Shaka converted as chief of the Zulus in 1816, the tribe totaled less than 1,500 and was between the smaller of the hundreds of other tribes in southern Africa. Nonetheless,

Shaka established a distinguished military organization. The entity formed well-commanded soldiers as he armed them with assegais, a new type of long-bladed, short weapon that was simple to operate deadly.

The Zulus quickly won nearby tribes, consolidating the survivors into their ranks—KwaZulu-Natal South Africa in July 1787. The Zulu triumphs exceedingly destabilized the area and finished in a vast flow of movements by extracted tribes. Shaka's mother, Nandi, passed away in 1827, then Shaka lost his mind. Nandi's death was extremely hard for Shaka. Shaka had experienced a mental illness that threatened to destroy the Zulu tribe. He caused hundreds of Zulus to get murdered and prevented planting vegetables and controlling milk for an entire cycle. All women with child and their spouses were targeted and put to death. Shaka commanded his troops on a very long military operation, causing them to return too fatigued and only to send them back out again. Shaka's very own half-brothers had no choice but to kill Shaka on September 22, 1828. Dingane took the slain King of Zulu's throne.

Lesson Learned:

_____

_____

_____

_____

MAYA INCA AZTEC CIVILIZATION

In 1168, the Maya people were obsessed with the Pleiades. Inca Olmec people Maya was the first to settle in Mexico. Without building significant cities, they became widespread and prosperous. They were the Aztecs and modern-day Mexico. Two other similarities between these three civilizations are using a calendar, which they used to predict eclipses, schedule religious ceremonies, determine when to plant/harvest crops, and go off to wars. They all had some form of a writing system. These three distinct groups adapted to their terrains where they lived. Olmecs lived near the Gulf of Mexico, and Mayas lived in today's Yucatan Peninsula of Mexico. Their priests were outstanding mathematicians and astronomers.

They developed a mathematics system with 20 as the base, accurate calendars, and were the first Native Americans that developed a writing system. The Aztecs lived in Central Mexico. They were a very progressive community because they built bridges, causeways, and canal networks. They had faith that their gods, which they worshipped, controlling their gardens and natural disaster.

The Mayas and Aztecs even performed human sacrifices to keep their gods pleased. The Aztecs used male prisoners of war for this practice. They all created gods sketched into carvings, figurines, carved stone murals, pottery, etc. They had a couple of similarities using calendars to predict the eclipse cycles and plan their religious ceremonies to know when to begin their gardening duties, including when to engage in war. All three of them had their own distinct writing system. Another significant difference between them was their farming methods. The Olmecs used the slash-and-burn farming method to clear the land by cutting down and burning trees. This would then enrich the soil. After a while, the ground would become exhausted, and the whole process would be executed on a fresh piece of land. They all lived in different locations, had various forms of government, used other farming methods, and each group worshiped a distinct god.

Lesson Learned:

_____

_____

_____

_____

_____

_____

_____

_____

_____

_____

KING SOLOMON

King Solomon, a Caucasian man, was the ruler known as the King of Israel. His mother was Bathsheba and King David. King Solomon is known for building the first Temple in Jerusalem. The last King of his father, *King David*, to reign power during a unified Israel. People traveled far miles to express their admiration and love for providing many different precious metals such as gold, silver, and herbs spices. *Queen of Sheba* came to verify his wisdom and stayed for six months. Solomon had a glass floor built before his throne to trick Makeda or Bilqīs, also referred to as Queen of Sheba, into thinking it was water, raised her skirts to cross it, and revealed that her legs were genuinely hairy. She returned to Ethiopia and conceived their son named **Melinek**, who became *the King of the Solomonic dynasty in Ethiopia*.

Willy lynch letter is a massively distributed testament to the extremes to break the unity and control by teaching wicked slave owner lynching and psychological techniques from his last name. It was penetrated throughout the world to make the slaves mentally weak by keeping the body healthy controlling the mind. It included grooming the black female slave into being dependent on him by displaying a taunting visual of pulling the black man apart from her, which embedded loneliness. Picnic - derived from the spectator activity pick a nigger would lynch a nigger racial, economic jealousy.

Lesson Learned:

_____

_____

_____

_____

_____

_____

Sherika Duncan

Abraham Lincoln

After 400 yrs. of slavery, the 16th President of the United States, Abraham Lincoln, *freed the slaves*. He was the President of the United States in 1861 and was assassinated in 1865. Through the American Civil War, Lincoln led the nation, the country's greatest moral, constitutional, and political crisis. The President was the first to have been assassinated. He was shot at the Ford's Theater in Washington, D.C. Then, the very next morning, at approximately 7:22 a.m. Lincoln died. This dreadful account happened only a week after the American Civil War ended.

Lesson Learned:

_____

_____

_____

_____

BLACK WALL STREET

Tulsa, Oklahoma home of the famous GAP band, is known for the Black Wallstreet, which housed nearly two hundred businesses. In the early 1900s - June 1, 1921, Tulsa's historic greenwood district, burn to the ground for twelve long hours by jealous Caucasians of the organization referred to as the KKK. There were approximately fifteen homes destroyed. Our glimpse of Africa's golden door of the black community on America's soil was diminished. An estimated $46-$1000 circulated in the year 1910 by successful business infrastructure. Six hundred black businesses covering thirty-six square block area included greenwood avenue and pine street.

Lesson Learned:

_____

_____

_____

_____

_____

_____

_____

_____

_____

HUMAN ZOO

Despite all the obstacles, we were still a thriving human zoo - feeding bananas - rabbit drops of blood. There has been nothing done to provide an official apology and no plans of creating future propaganda to change the negative image to state they were wrong when they enslaved our people. We were punished because our genetically designed organs and skin are better on the genetic level. The forced integration of white dominance and stereotype make themselves believe they were genetically better than us. It is when the new wave of the world fair, circuses, and 'freak shows began.

Can you see the lockdown as being a sense of imprisonment?

If so, you are ascending.

OTA BENGA

In 1906, Dr. Samuel P. Verner purchased Benga relocated him from Africa. He orchestrated a human exhibit at the Bronx Zoo the 23 years old, 4 feet 11 inches, weighing in at 103 pounds, Ota Benga from Kasai River, Congo Free State, South Central Africa, for display each day for September. Benga remained in the United States in the state of Virginia for his entire life. Various Blacked owned newspapers around the United States opposed his treatment. They formed a petition to the New York City Mayor, George McClellan, to release Benga from the Bronx Zoo. In the later part of 1906, Benga was released to an orphanage in Brooklyn called Howard Colored Orphan Asylum to *James M. Gordon,* the supervisor. Mr. Gordon allowed him to live in Virginia, where he received tutoring in English and worked in the tobacco factory. In 1910, during the World War I Benga was severely depressed and committed suicide.

Lesson Learned:

_____

_____

_____

_____

_____

_____

_____

_____

_____

_____

DR. MARTIN L. KING, JR.

Photo by Robert Abbott Sengstacke via Getty Images

In 1963, the Freedom march was organized with Bayard Rustin, an openly gay man, to start the civil rights movement agenda. Allegedly, the FBI had a lot of dirt on Dr. Martin Luther King, Jr. Jacqueline Kennedy said to Bobby Kennedy the FBI had tapes of Dr. King buying hookers cheated multiple times and had orgies. But they wanted Dr. Martin Luther King, Jr. to succeed. Unfortunately, he started to go against what the FBI wanted him to do. So, they sent the tape to Coretta King.

Lesson Learned:

_____

_____

_____

_____

_____

_____

_____

_____

_____

_____

PUBLIC HOUSING PLAN & DRUGS

In the late 1970s, building a tall building in poverty-stricken neighborhoods than a year later mid-80s, the CIA placed drugs in the black community. Freeway Ricky Ross and the Walmart of crack, Leroy Chico Brown was selling crack cocaine in Los Angeles to Crips and Blood in south-central. During the 1980s, the Cops TV show and hip hop were in full effect.

Lesson Learned:

_____

_____

_____

_____

MALCOM X

Malcolm X changed his last name after being released from jail because Little was forced upon his ancestors by Caucasian owners as a sign of slavery. The X symbolized his unknown African family name. Malcolm X, also known as his Muslim name of El-hajj Malik El Shabazz. Rumors circulated that he was assassinated by the Nation of Islam.

Lesson Learned:

___

___

___

___

___

DR. WESLEY MUHAMMAD

In his book, Dr. Wesley Muhammad describes "Black Arabia & The African Origin of Islam" how the illuminating light's iridescence caused God to appear as a blue-black God. The black skin, even in the darkness, displays light. In our original forms, we take on as dark gods because we always admit light, even feeling light. Because all things are light, and all things made in existence provides an ultraviolet radiance of light to the point where you don't see it. There are levels to your darkness and to your understanding of night. You must be rooted and grounded in enlightenment to attract all beings. You must always protect yourself and your energies.

Lesson Learned:

_____

_____

_____

References

https://theafricanhistory.com/1274
https://www.history.com/news/solomon-northup-after-his-12-years-a-slave
https://www.pbs.org/wgbh/aia/part1/1p272.html
http://abolition.e2bn.org/people_35.html
https://chapter18africa.weebly.com/mansa-musa.html
https://theafricanhistory.com/224
https://www.mayaincaaztec.com/ancient-civilizations/olmec-civilization
https://www.nationalgeographic.org/media/kingdoms-kush/
https://critograph.com/2017/09/14/ota-benga-honored/
https://www.biography.com/political-figure/alexander-the-great
http://www.baytagoodah.com/uploads/9/5/6/0/95600058/308769687-black-arabia.pdf

LEAVE A REVIEW AND PURCHASE OTHER BOOKS DIRECTLY ON WWW.SHERIKADUNCAN.COM

THE SETUP NOVEL

SOUL YOU BOOK COLLECTION
Soul You Vol I: The Grand Awakening
Soul You Vol. II: The Procreator
Soul You Vol III: The Protector
Soul You Vol. IV: Scribble Journal

media@sherikaduncan.com

Copyright © 2021 Sherika Duncan Enterprise

All rights reserved.

www.ingramcontent.com/pod-product-compliance
Lightning Source LLC
Chambersburg PA
CBHW062205100526
44589CB00014B/1962